Habitat Homes

Jean Feldman and Holly Karapetkova

Tune: Home on the Range

www.rourkeclassroom.com

Oh, give me a home, a dry desert home,

Where the sun shines most every day.

Cacti and yucca plants,

Lizards, camels, and ants,

Call the desert habitat home.

Cacti

Yucca

Lizard

Camel

Oh, give me a home, a tropical home,

Where it rains almost every day.

Vines, ferns, and green trees,

Parrots and chimpanzees,

Call the rainforest habitat home.

Vine

Fern

Parrots

Chimpanzee

Oh, give me a home, a white arctic home,

Where it's icy and cold every day.

Polar bears, caribou,

Walrus, seals, and whales, too,

Call the arctic habitat home.

Polar Bear

Caribou

Walruses

Whale

Oh, give me a home, a tall woodlands home,

Where the trees stand strong every day.

Maples, oaks, elms, and deer,

Birds and squirrels all live here,

Call the woodlands habitat home.

Maple

Oak

Elm

Deer

Home, sweet habitat homes,

Where the plants and the animals roam.

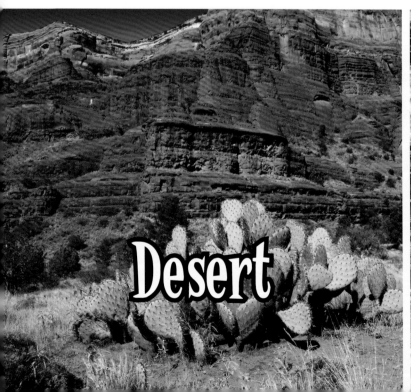

Desert

Tropical

They're comfortable here,

Anytime of the year,

Arctic

Woodland

They're adapted to their habitat homes.